beads & buttons

erika knight

beads & buttons

25 simple jewellery projects
to instruct and inspire

erika knight

QUADRILLE

We all love to collect things on our travels: a shell from a beach, daisies from a meadow, an odd button parted from a garment. These talismans and treasures are often put aside, saved for no apparent reason other than the way they glistened and caught our eye, how they felt in our hand or as the physical embodiment of a moment, place or time.

Most creators are natural magpies, collecting and secreting away precious pieces for future projects. I have fond memories of much-loved needlework classes at primary school. Each pupil was allocated a brown cardboard box, on which a coloured paper square boldly displayed our name in handwritten script. Inside were pieces of gingham, binca and felt, ready for our next craft venture. What we all really hankered after, however, was glitter.

My classmates traded shiny remnants of satin, slivers of silky thread and special gems like buttons and beads; this was the usual covert mission that occupied much of each lesson. I still remember and embrace that spirit: the personal pleasure gained from tiny bits and pieces, nothing of any real practical use, but treasures nonetheless.

This simple introduction to beads and buttons, brings you individual ideas and projects to make from those treasures. With 25 different jewellery designs, this book includes show-stopping, yet unashamedly easy-to-make pieces.

This book has also afforded me a long-awaited opportunity to work with Joy Fox, a craft maker of rare distinction, whose ambient style is at once beautiful and accessible. On first glance her work appears elegantly simple, but the difference is in the detail. Each design is so well thought through – from her exquisite selection of materials, tones and textures, to the balance of each design – showing the purity of her perfected techniques.

Joy Fox studied fine art and followed with a career in graphic design, but in this technological world she missed the 'hands-on' approach of craft. So Joy began to create one-off jewellery pieces, transforming the discarded into something utterly beautiful: most of the materials she uses are recycled, found in markets or thrift shops.

Joy's button jewellery designs developed from a necklace that she made for herself; reminiscent of a daisy chain, it comprised of odd mother-of-pearl buttons strung simply onto some leather thonging. She got so many favourable comments, she decided to develop the idea into a jewellery range.

When looking at Joy's work, many people are taken back to their childhood, playing with Grandma's tin of buttons. Her pieces can appear nostalgic, but they can also take on a more contemporary edge, depending on the buttons selected. Her work is exhibited in discerning craft galleries across the UK and Eire.

materials & techniques

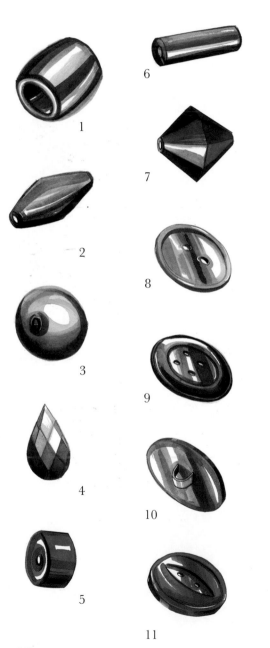

beads and buttons

Some of the vast array of bead and button shapes available are shown left. They are made from a huge variety of materials as well. Simply use the new or vintage beads and buttons that you like; choose them for colour, texture and shape. Using multiples of the same-style bead or button can create a simple but very effective design.

type

1 pony bead

2 lampwork bead

3 ball bead

4 drop bead

5 seed bead

6 bugle bead

7 crystal bead

8 two-hole button

9 four-hole button

10 shank button

11 fisheye button

threads and cords

Just about anything goes for thread or cord. As long as it can pass through the bead or button, then any continuous length of string, linen, hemp, wire, leather, suede, ribbon, velvet, fabric strips, nylon, lurex and any other yarn you can think of can be used for a design. Simply experiment.

type

1 linen
2 hemp
3 ribbon

4 round leather cord
5 flat suede cord
6 wire

1

2

3

4

5

6

11

threading

When choosing the materials for a project, make sure your chosen thread will go through the holes or shanks in all the beads and buttons that you plan to use, especially where a design requires the thread to pass through the hole or shank twice or more.

Any necklace or bracelet can be made either shorter or longer, simply cut the thread to the length required and use fewer or more beads and buttons.

Always overestimate a little on the thread.

creating a slanted thread

Use a pair of sharp scissors to cut the end of the thread into a slanted point to make it easier to thread through holes and shanks.

using a bradawl

Use the tip of a fine bradawl to ease through any stubborn threads that will not easily go through a hole or shank.

threading a four-hole button

When threading a four-hole button, thread through the 'diagonal' and back through the last hole so that the button will lie flat.

knotting

I have used only the simplest of techniques to create the projects in this book – limited to just three types of knots.

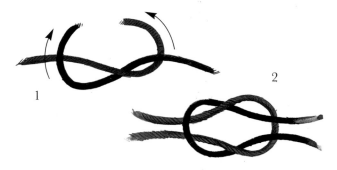

slip knot

1 Make a loop in the tail end of the yarn, crossing the tail end of the yarn over the ball end. Let the tail end drop down behind the loop, then catch the tail end and pull it through the loop.

2 Holding the tail end and the ball end of the yarn in your left hand, pull the loop in the opposite direction to create a tight knot.

reef knot

1 Take the thread end coming in from the left over the thread end coming in from the right.and then behind it.

2 Take the two ends above the crossed threads and take the thread that is now coming in from the right over the thread coming in from the left and behind it. Pull the thread ends in the opposite direction to create a tight knot.

loop knot

1 Fold the yarn in half to create a loop end. take the thread ends up and over the loop end to create a loop, then pass the thread ends behind and through the loop. Pull the loop end and thread ends in the opposite direction to create a tight knot.

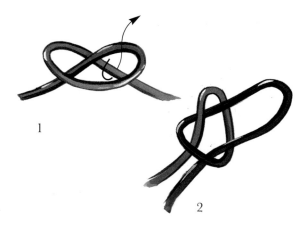

13

making a tassel

Tassels are a great way to decorate a project, adding instant glamour and elegance. They are easy to make yet effective, and can be a real feature in a piece, such as the necklace on page 118.

1 Cut a square piece of cardboard to the desired length of the tassel. Wrap yarn around and around the cardboard. Take a separate strand of yarn, insert it at the top edge between the cardboard and the wrapped yarn and tie it securely. Cut the wrapped strands at the lower edge.

2 Take another strand of yarn and wrap it around and around the top end of the tassel to create a shank. Create a loop at one end of this length, secure it to the tassel with a couple of wraps of the yarn, then once the yarn has been wrapped the desired amount of times around the tassel, thread the other end through the loop and pull tight to secure. Trim any uneven strands for a neat finish.

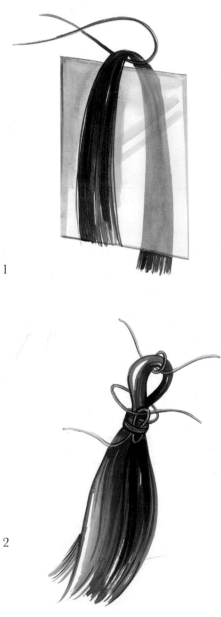

1

2

making a pompon

Like tassels, pompons are simple to create and good for adding decorative detail to a project, such as the necklace on page 66. When tying the pompon, do make sure that it is tightly bound so that it will not easily pull apart or disintegrate.

1 Cut two identical circles of cardboard that are slightly smaller than the size of the pompon you need. Cut a hole in the centre of each one and hold the circles together. Thread a blunt-ended yarn needle with yarn and wind it continually through the centre and outer edges until the hole has closed.

2 Insert the tips of the scissors between the two circles and cut the yarn around the cardboard circles.

3 Tie a piece of yarn tightly between the two cardboard circles. Remove the cardboard, cutting through them if necessary. Trim any uneven strands for a neat finish.

1

2

3

wrapping a bead in fabric

You can use a variety of printed or embellished fabrics to wrap a bead, making this a unique and inexpensive way to personalise and even coordinate your accessories.

1 Cut a square piece of fabric large enough to entirely wrap around your chosen bead.

2 Spray the wrong side of the fabric with PVA adhesive. Wrap the fabric around the bead so that the two side edges meet, trimming if necessary.

3 Slightly twist the top and bottom ends of fabric, rather like a sweet wrapper, trimming and tucking any excess into the bead's hole using a fine knitting needle or bradawl.

1

2

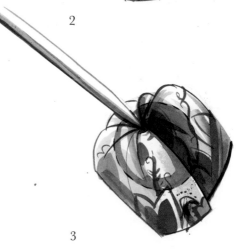

3

crochet cast on

When beginning to crochet you must work a foundation chain, which will form the basis of the fabric, but first you must tie a slip knot onto the hook and find a comfortable position for holding the hook and yarn.

slip knot

Make a loop in the tail end of the yarn, crossing the tail end over the ball end. Let the tail end drop down behind the loop, then pass the crochet hook over the loop on the right, catch the tail end with the hook and pull it through the loop. Holding the tail end and the ball end in your left hand, pull the hook in the opposite direction to create the first loop on the hook. There will be a tight knot under it.

starting to crochet

To crochet easily and successfully, you need to hold the yarn and the hook comfortably, with enough tension on the yarn, so that when you draw the hook around the yarn, it stays firmly in the lip of the hook. Most people choose to wrap the yarn around their fingers, and some make an additional wrap around their little finger – choose whichever yarn-holding method works best for you.

Similarly, hold the hook in whichever way you find most comfortable. Some people favour a pencil grip, while others hold the hook between their tumb and forefinger like a knife. You may even prefer to change your grip, depending on the type of stitch you are working at the time or on the size of the hook.

foundation chain

After you have made the slip knot on your hook, the next step is to create the foundation chain for the crochet fabric. The project instructions will tell you how many chain stitches to make to start. The abbreviation for chain is 'ch'.

1 With the slip knot on the hook, grip the tail end of the yarn between thumb and forefinger of your left hand. Holding the working yarn taut in your left hand, pass the tip of the hook in front of the yarn, then under and around it. Catch the yarn in the lip of the hook.

2 Draw the yarn through the loop on the hook. This completes the first chain and leaves one loop on the hook.

3 To make the next chain, pull a new loop through the loop on the hook. Make the number of chains required, keeping the stitches slightly loose so you can work into them easily on your first row.

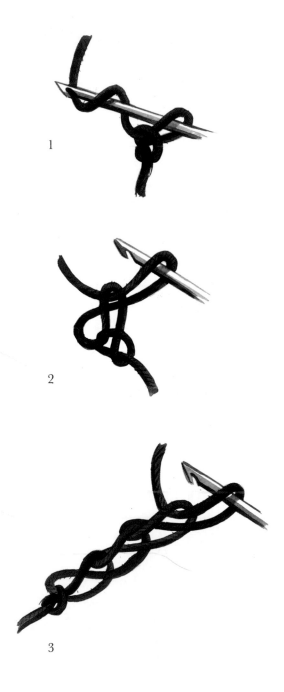

1

2

3

slip stitch crochet

Slip stitch is also known as 'single crochet'. When worked into the foundation chain and continued in rows, slip stitches form a dense, unyielding fabric. They are more commonly used to join the end and beginning of a round, or to work invisibly along the top of other stitches until you reach the required position.

Make a foundation chain of the required number of chains. Insert the tip of the hook through the second chain from the hook, then catch the yarn with the hook (called 'wrap the yarn around the hook') and draw it through both the chain and the loop on the hook. This completes the first slip stitch and leaves one loop on the hook. Work the next slip stitch into the next chain in the same way. Continue as required.

double crochet

Double crochet creates a dense yet flexible fabric, which is ideal for hardwearing, strong textiles. The easiest of all crochet fabrics to make, it is used frequently.

1 Make the number of foundation chain you require. Insert the hook into the second chain from the hook. Wrap the yarn around the hook and pull a loop through the chain. There are now two loops on the hook.

2 Wrap the yarn around the hook and draw a loop through both loops on the hook. This completes the first double.

3 To make the next double, insert the hook through the next chain, draw a loop through, then draw the a loop through both loops on the hook. Work a double into each of the remaining chains in the same way to complete the first row.

4 To start any subsequent rows of double, turn the work so the loop on the hook is at the right-hand edge. Make a turning chain to take the yarn up to the correct height by drawing a loop through the loop on the hook to form a loose chain. Inserting the hook through both loops at the top of the first stitch in the row below, work a double into each double of the previous row.

1

2

3

4

1

2

3

4

treble crochet

Treble crochet is taller than double crochet. It results in a stitch that is more open and less dense, so it is a flexible soft textile. It is worked in the same way as a double crochet, except that you wrap the yarn around the hook before beginning the stitch. The abbreviation used for treble crochet is 'tr'.

1 Make the number of foundation chain you require. Then wrap the yarn around the hook.

2 Insert the hook into the fourth chain from the hook, wrap the yarn around the hook and pull a loop through the chain. There are now three loops on the hook.

3 Wrap the yarn around the hook and draw a loop through the first two loops on the hook. There are now two loops on the hook.

4 Wrap the yarn around the hook and draw it through the remaining two loops on the hook. This completes the first treble. Work a treble into each of the remaining chains in the same way to complete the first row. To start any subsequent rows, turn the work, then work three chains to count as the first treble. Miss the first treble in the row below and work a treble into the next treble. Work a treble into each remaining treble to the end of the row, then work the last treble into the third of the three chains at the end.

1

2

3

4

knitting cast-on

When beginning to knit, first work a foundation row called a cast-on. The method shown here is the thumb cast-on. It produces a flexible edge that is useful when using non-elastic yarns such as cotton.

1 Estimate the length of yarn needed to cast on the required amount of stitches. If unsure, allow for more yarn than you think you need as you can use what is left over for sewing up. Make a slip knot on a knitting needle (see page 17), leaving a long tail end. With the slip knot on the needle in your right hand and the yarn that comes from the ball over your forefinger, wrap the tail end of the yarn over your left thumb from front to back, holding the yarn in your palm with your fingers.

2 Insert the knitting needle upwards through the yarn loop on your left thumb.

3 With the right forefinger, wrap the yarn from the ball up and over the point of the knitting needle.

4 Draw the yarn through the loop on your thumb to form a new stitch on the knitting needle. Then, let the yarn loop slip off your left thumb and pull the loose end to tighten up the stitch. Repeat these steps until the required number of stitches have been cast on.

knit stitch

The knit and purl stitches form the basis of almost all knitted fabrics. When the knit stitch is worked continuously it forms a reversible fabric called garter stitch, which is used in the silver cuff with turquoise beads (see page 40).

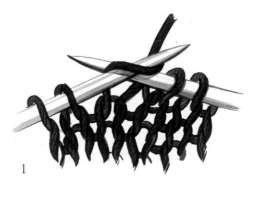

1 With the cast-on stitches on the needle in your left hand, insert the right-hand needle from left to right and from front to back through the first cast-on stitch.

2 Take the yarn from the ball on your forefinger (the working yarn) around the point of the right-hand needle.

3 Draw the right-hand needle and yarn through the stitch, thus forming a new stitch on the right-hand needle, and at the same time slip the original stitch off the left-hand needle. Repeat these steps until all the stitches from the left-hand needle have been worked. One knit row has now been completed.

purl stitch

After the knit stitch, move on to the purl stitch. If you work the purl stitch continuously it forms the same fabric as garter stitch. However, if you alternate the purl rows with knit rows, it creates stocking stitch.

1 With the yarn to the front of the work, insert the right-hand needle from the right to the left into the front of the first stitch on the left-hand needle.

2 Then take the yarn from the ball on your forefinger (the working yarn) around the point of the right-hand needle.

3 Draw the right-hand needle and the yarn through the stitch, thus forming a new stitch on the right-hand needle, and at the same time slip the original stitch off the left-hand needle. Repeat these steps until all the stitches have been worked. One purl row has now been completed.

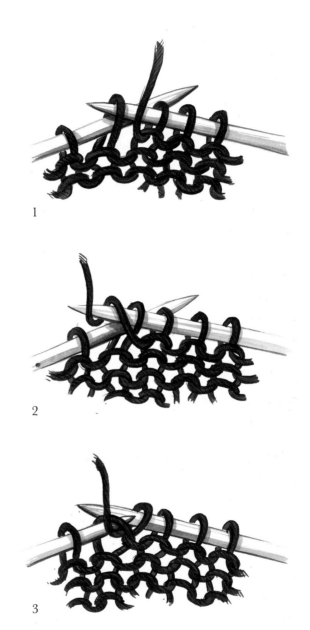

1

2

3

knitting cast off

Casting off is used to finish a knitted piece so the stitches don't unravel. Unless told otherwise, cast off in the pattern used.

knit cast-off

1 Knit two stitches. Insert left-hand needle into first stitch knitted on right-hand needle and lift over second stitch and off right-hand needle.

2 One stitch is now on right-hand needle. Knit next stitch. Repeat first step until all stitches have been cast off. Pull yarn through last stitch to fasten off.

purl cast-off

1 Purl two stitches. Insert left-hand needle into first stitch worked on right-hand needle and lift over second stitch and off right-hand needle.

2 One stitch is now on right-hand needle. Purl next stitch. Repeat first step until all stitches have been cast off. Pull yarn through last stitch to fasten off.

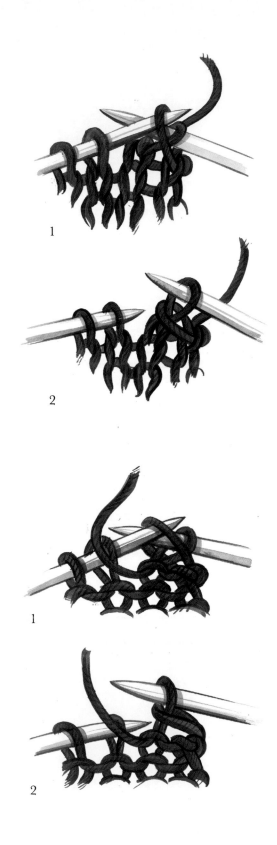

1

2

1

2

knitting grafting

This is an invisible method of joining two pieces of knitting with the stitches either on or off the needles.

1 Place pieces to be joined close together, with the stitches on each piece corresponding to those opposite. Thread a blunt-ended yarn needle with matching yarn. Starting at the right edge of knitting, bring needle up through the first stitch of the lower piece from back to front, then through the first stitch of the upper piece from back to front. Bring it down through the first stitch of the lower piece from front to back and bring it up again through the next stitch to the left from back to front.

2 On the upper piece, pass the needle down from front to back through the same stitch it came up through before and bring it up from back to front through the next stitch to the left. If working with stitches still on the needles, slip them off one by one as they are secured.

3 On the lower piece, take the needle down from front to back through the stitch it came up through before and bring It up through the next stitch to the left from back to front. Repeat in the same way to the end, keeping the tension the same as the knitted fabric. Weave in the loose ends at the back of the work when completed, or run into a seam if possible.

natural

stone, silver & suede pendant

materials

1m green suede thread, 3mm thick

A 1 x large (35mm) stone with naturally eroded or
    drilled hole

B 2 x small (15mm) silver disks

cut a 100cm length of thread. **tie** a loop knot (see page 13) at one end to create a 5–6cm loop which will form the fastener. **thread** one of the silver disks (B). **thread** the large stone (A). **tie** the second silver disk onto the thread at the other end using a reef knot (see page 13) to complete the fastening.

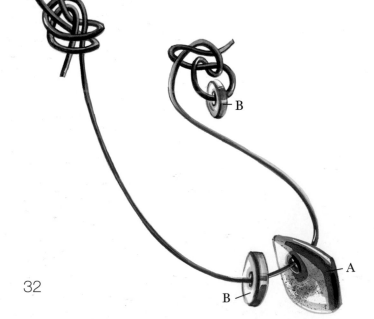

horn button & amber glass bead bracelet

Chunky natural horn buttons are topped with amber glass beads to produce a simple and stylish accessory.

horn button and amber glass bead bracelet

materials

1m brown mercerised
    cotton thread (bootlace)

A 8 x large (25mm) two-
    hole horn buttons

B 7 x small (5mm) amber
    glass faceted bugle
    beads

C 1 x large (25mm) four-
    hole horn button

D 1 x small (20mm) two-
    hole horn/wood button

bradawl

PVA adhesive

notes • it takes a while to get a feel for the twine and its tension • cut the end of the thread into a slanted point to make it easier to thread through the buttons.

cut an 85cm length of cotton thread. **fold** in half to find the centre. **thread** the first button (A) from the back over the two ends and move towards the folded centre. Do not thread right up to the centre but leave enough at the folded end to create a 5–6cm loop which will form the fastener. **hold** the loop and button in one hand, take the first strand and feed it back through the opposite hole. **take** the second strand, thread a bead (B) and feed it back through the other hole. **check** the tension as you go.

thread up through second button (A), making sure that second button slightly overlaps the first button. **add** bead (B), thread back through second button. **repeat** until last button. **finish** with a four-hole button (C), add bead (D), and cross-stitch. **tie** off with a reef knot (see page 13) on the diagonal so that it lies flatly and neatly. **trim** the ends. **dab** knot and ends with PVA adhesive. **allow** to dry.

leather, turquoise & silver bead necklace

materials

1m leather thonging
A 10 x small (10mm) turquoise beads
B 8 x small (6mm) silver flat disks
PVA adhesive

cut a 100cm length of leather thonging. **fold** in half to find the centre. **tie** a loop knot (see page 13) at the point where you want to fix the overhead loop. **take** one thread end and thread the first bead (A). No need to knot. **thread** a disk (B) followed by another bead. **repeat** until you have threaded five beads alternating with four disks. **tie** the thread ends with a simple knot. **repeat** the threading for the other side using the second end. **trim** the thread ends. **dab** both knots and ends with PVA adhesive. **allow** to dry..

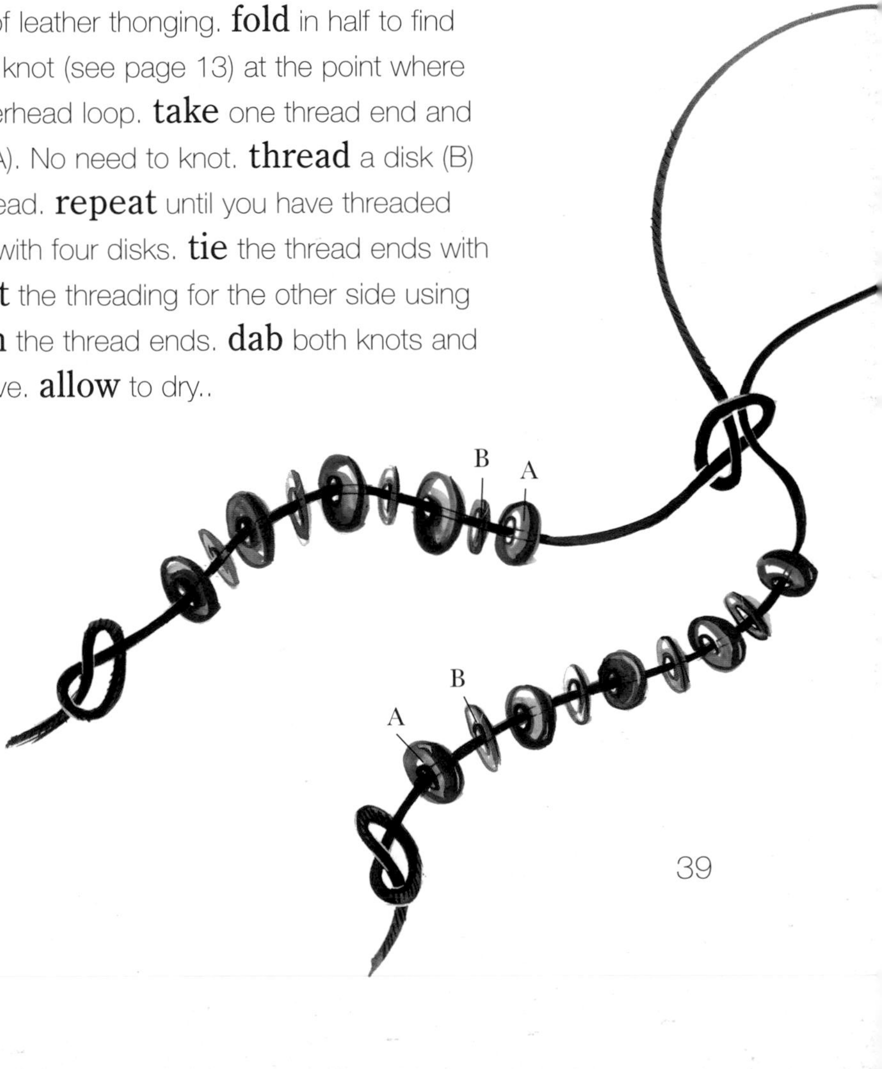

B   A

B

A

knitted wire & turquoise bead cuff

A decorative cuff worked in silver wire with semi-precious natural turquoise stones. The cuff is knitted in wire in garter stitch. It consists of two bracelets made in different weight wire – one worked with beads – and then joined around the edge.

notes • for basic instructions on how to knit, see pages 24–29 • when knitting in the beads, only add them on every alternate row to ensure that all the beads sit on the same side of the work

make the under bracelet. **cast** on 9 stitches using the 0.6mm gauge wire and 5mm knitting needles. **work** in garter stitch (knit every row) until bracelet measures 21.5cm when stretched. **cast** off by grafting the cast-on edge to the cast-off edge (see page 29).

make the top bracelet. **thread** the beads onto the 0.4mm gauge wire. **cast** on 10 stitches using the threaded 0.4mm gauge wire and 5mm knitting needles. **work** in garter stitch as before but add the beads to the knitting randomly. **add** a bead: put the right-hand needle through the next stitch on the left-hand needle, slide the bead along the wire as close as possible to your work, then knit the stitch in the normal way. **work** until bracelet measures 21.5cm when stretched. **cast** off by grafting the cast-on edge to the cast-off edge as before.

finish by placing the under bracelet inside the top bracelet. **oversew** together at the top and bottom with lengths of fine wire, ensuring that all loose ends are woven in.

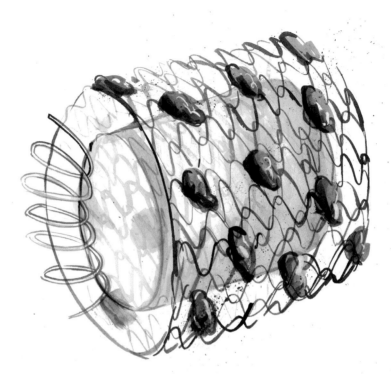

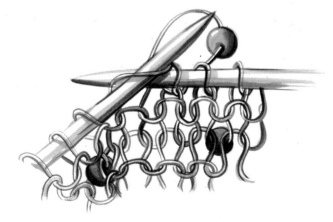

materials

For under bracelet:

1 x 10m pack silver wire,
  0.6mm gauge

5mm knitting needles

For top bracelet:

1 x 20m pack silver wire,
  0.4mm gauge

28 x medium (15–20mm) semi-
  precious turquoise beads

5mm knitting needles

crochet motif & mirror bead necklace

An assymetrical necklace, this accessory is made of crochet motifs in natural hemp yarn and embellished with small glass beads, sequins and contrasting faceted stones. A simple twisted tie and loop fastens the necklace together with a natural button.

note • for basic instructions on crochet, see pages 17–23
• this design is asymmetric, but you may wish to rearrange
the motifs to give a more symmetrical design

make two large flowers. **base ring** using yarn and hook,
make 12 ch and join into ring with a slip stitch. **round 1** 1 ch,
18 dc in ring, slip stitch to first dc. **round 2** 1 ch, 1 dc in
same dc as 1-ch, 3 ch, miss 2 dc, [1 dc in next dc, 3 ch, miss
2 dc] 5 times, slip stitch to first dc. **round 3** 1 ch, [in next
3-ch loop work 1 dc, 3 ch, 3 tr, 3 ch, 1 dc] 6 times, slip stitch
to first dc. **fasten off** leaving a long tail end for joining motifs.
make second large flower but with beads. **thread** 42
beads (A) onto yarn. **work** as for first flower but add a bead
to every dc in rounds 1 and 2 and every tr in round 3.

make two small beaded circles. **thread** 18 beads (A) onto
yarn. **work** base ring and round 1 of large flower, adding a
bead on every dc of round 1. **fasten off** leaving a long tail
end for joining motifs. **make** the second circle the same.

make one medium flower. **thread** 6 beads (A) onto yarn.
work base ring, round 1 and round 2 of large flower, adding
a bead on the second chain of each 3-chain loop of round 2.
fasten off leaving a long tail end for joining motifs.

arrange the necklace. **place** one small circle first, followed
by one medium flower, two large flowers and one small circle.
sew the motifs together in this order with a few sewing stitches,

using the long tail ends of yarn. **decorate** the flower motifs
with sequins (B), securing some in place with a holding bead (C).
add the larger faceted beads (D).

cut a length of yarn 60cm long. **twist** the yarn tightly, then fold
in half and let strands twist together. **knot** the end without the
fold. **loop** folded end onto one small beaded circle. **tie** button
(F) to other end. **make** a second cord in the same way, but
make a loop at the end for fastening to the button (E).

materials

1 x 50g ball double-knitting-
   weight natural hemp yarn,
   such as Lanaknits Hemp
   Natural Hemp6
2.5mm crochet hook
A 84 x small (3mm) glass
   seed beads
B 12 x small (5mm) silver
   sequins
C 6 x small (3mm) holding beads
D 3 x medium (8–10mm)
   faceted mirror beads
E 1 x medium (15mm)
   mother-of-pearl button
sewing needle and thread

double bone button choker

This design is worked with numerous buttons of the same size and colour. The result is an articulated necklace, which curves and sits around the neck beautifully.

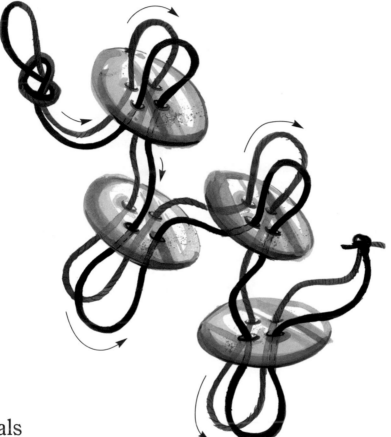

materials

1.5m ecru mercerised
cotton thread (bootlace)
50 x medium (17mm) four-
hole bone buttons
PVA adhesive

notes • it is important to use the same size and thickness of buttons throughout

cut a 150cm length of cotton thread, or three times the length of the choker you require. **fold** in half to find the centre. **leave** enough at the folded end to create a 5–6cm loop which will form the fastener. **make** a simple loop knot (see page 13). **thread** the first button over the two ends and move towards the loop knot. **turn** first button over and thread a second button, making sure that second button slightly overlaps the first button. **turn** again and thread a third button in the same way. **repeat** until last button. **tie** off with a reef knot (see page 13) on the diagonal so that it lies flatly and neatly. **trim** the ends. **dab** knot and ends with PVA adhesive. **allow** to dry.

linen, glass bead & button necklace

materials

1.5m linen or hemp thread

A 12–14 x small (35mm) assorted buttons, such as
   mother-of-pearl, glass and bone

B 7–8 x small (15mm) clear glass faceted bugle beads

PVA adhesive

cut a 150cm length of linen thread. **arrange** the assorted beads and buttons in the order you want to thread them. **take** the thread end and the first button (A) or bugle bead (B) and thread through, tieing a simple knot if necessary to prevent it from slipping. **leave** a large space and tie a simple knot. **thread** the next bead or button and again tie a simple knot if necessary, then leave a large space as before. **continue** in this way until the necklace is the length required.

finish with a four-hole button, take the thread end up through the back of the button and then down again. thread back up throught the button diagonally (see page 12). **tie** off with a reef knot (see page 13) on the diagonal so that it lies flatly and neatly. **trim** the ends. **dab** the knot and ends with PVA adhesive. **allow** to dry.

A

B

beachcomber bangles & earrings

Gathered small natural pieces are threaded onto silver wire, natural linen or fine coloured leather to create simple yet stylish summer accessories.

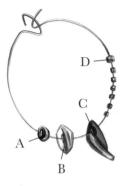

make two earrings to the same design. **assemble** the selected materials, making sure holes are large enough to thread. **bend** a little loop or 'eye' into one end of the wire using the pliers. **thread** the pearl bead (A), followed by the silver washer (B), then the mother-of-pearl piece (C) and finally the small glass beads (D). **bend** the end of the wire over carefully to create a 'hook' using the pliers.

assemble the selected materials, making sure holes are large enough to thread. **thread** the mother-of-pearl piece (A) onto the jump ring (B). **thread** all the pieces in turn onto the wire, make sure each end of the wire passes through each item. **adjust** wire to length required. **twist** the ends crossing and wrapping to give a decorative detail each side of the beads. **trim** the ends.

materials

for the wire earrings:
2 x lengths fine silver wire,
each approximately 15cm long
jewellery pliers
A 1 x small pearl bead
B 1 x silver flat washer
C 1 x mother-of-pearl piece
D approximately 13 x tiny
   turquoise glass beads

for the wire bracelet:
1 x length fine silver wire,
approximately 35cm long
jewellery pliers
A 1 x mother-of-pearl piece
B 1 x silver jump ring
C 1 x silver flat washer
D 1 x large turquoise glass
   bead

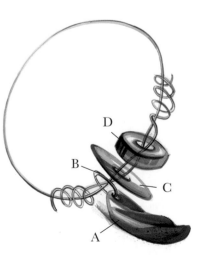

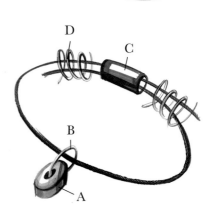

make a circle with the leather thonging, overlapping the ends. **tie** a reef knot (see page 13). **thread** a ornate silver bead on each end of the knot. **fasten** the end to the bracelet with a few twists of the silver wire, crossing and wrapping to create a decorative detail. **trim** the ends.

thread the turquoise bead onto the jump ring. **thread** the jump ring onto the linen thread. **thread** the coconut shell bead on to the linen thread. **make** a circle with the linen thread by overlapping the ends. **pass** both ends through the coconut shell bead. **fasten** each end of the linen yarn with a few twists of silver wire, crossing and wrapping to create a decorative detail. **trim** ends.

for leather bracelet:
1 x length silver leather thonging, approximately 35cm long
A 2 x ornate silver beads
B 2 x small lengths of fine
  silver wire

for the linen bracelet:
1 x length linen thread, approximately 35cm long
A 1 x natural turquoise bead
B 1 x silver jump ring
C 1 x natural coconut shell
  bugle bead
D 2 x small lengths of fine
  silver wire
jewellery pliers

57

wooden & pearl bead twisted rope necklace

Natural seed pearl beads and three sizes of wooden beads are threaded and knotted in long strands, twisted together and fastened with two modern silver coloured snap hooks to create a contemporary rope necklace. Use coloured beads as an alternative to the pearls as natural and colour work equally well together.

wooden and pearl bead twisted rope necklace

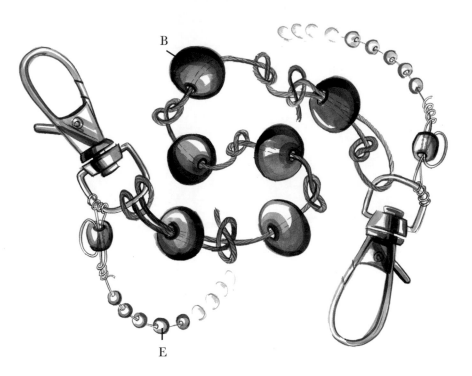

materials

6m linen thread

3m strong cotton thread

A 28 x large (30mm) wooden ball beads

B 30 x medium (25mm) wooden ball beads

C 90 x small (20mm) wooden ball beads

D 4 x silver beads (20mm)

E 150 x small (10mm) natural pearl seed beads

2 x silver coloured snap hooks

note • keep cutting the thread end diagonally to give a sharp point for easy threading • choose a strong cotton thread that will go through the small pearl holes • each necklace strand measures 71cm • use lengths of thread much longer than required, to allow for the knots

cut a 150cm length of linen thread. **fold** over one end of the thread and make a slip knot (see page 13) through the base ring of a snap hook. **thread** a large wooden bead (A) right over the loose end of the slip knot to cover it. **tie** a simple knot to secure the bead in position. **thread** more large wooden beads, knotting each into position, until strand measures 71cm. **work** a second strand using medium wooden beads (B) and a two more strands using small wooden beads (C). **thread** the four strand ends through the base ring of the second snap hook and then back through the last wooden bead on each strand and knot again.

cut a 150cm length of strong cotton thread. **fold** over one end of the thread and make a slip knot through the base ring of the snap hook as before. **thread** a silver bead (D) followed by 75 pearl beads (E) and finish with another silver bead. **thread** the end of the strong cotton thread through the base ring of the second snap hook and then back through the last silver bead several times to fasten off. **thread** a second strand of pearl beads and tie off in the same way. **twist** the necklace strands several times before fastening to create the twisted rope effect.

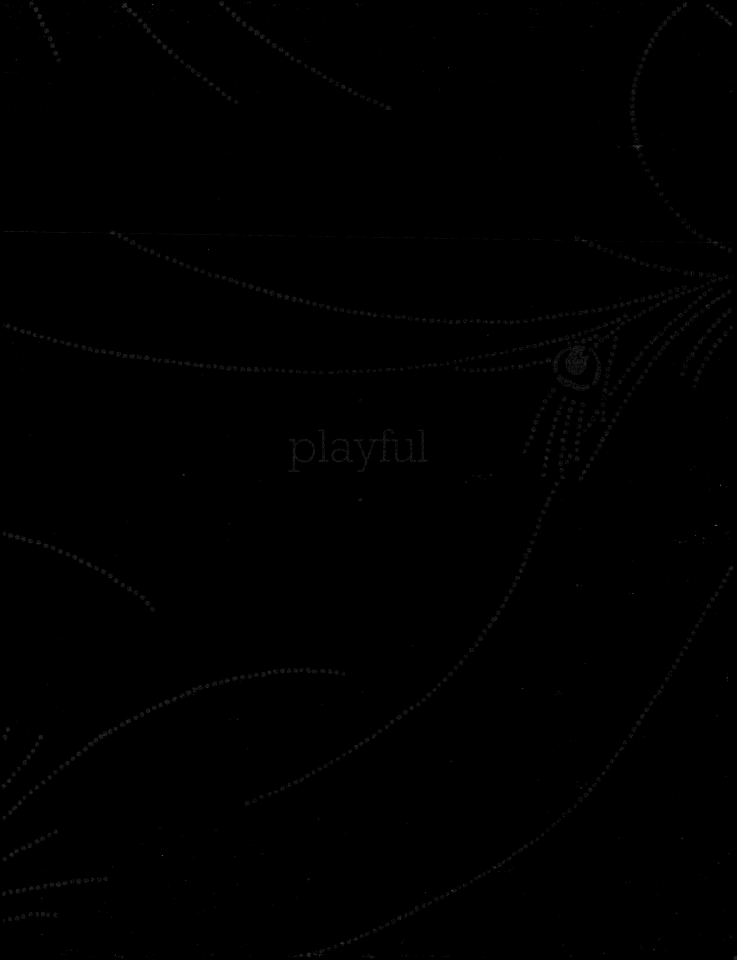

playful

knotted silk & wooden bead necklace

materials

approximately 0.5m printed silk fabric, 115cm wide
A 3 x large (30mm) wooden ball beads
B 6 x medium (25mm) wooden ball beads
C 3 x small (20mm) wooden ball beads
sewing needle and thread

make a fabric tube. cut three strips of fabric 10.5cm wide. join the strips to make one continuous strip. fold the fabric strip in half lengthwise, with right sides together, pin and tack. sew a 0.5cm seam all along the length. turn right side out.

mark the centre of the fabric tube by folding in half and knotting. insert one bead (A) into the tube and work towards the centre. twist the fabric and tie with a simple knot. insert another bead (A) either side of the first bead (A). twist the fabric and knot as before. insert three beads (B) on each side of the necklace, twisting and knotting as before. insert two beads (C) on each side of the necklace, twisting and knotting as before. tie the ends of the necklace into a large sash bow. trim the ends of the fabric tube, turn in and hand sew neatly.

linen wrapped beads & pompons necklace

A long rope necklace made of same-size wooden beads covered in linen yarn in a palette of washed pinks, wheat, lichen and claret. Each is knotted into position and the rope is trimmed with yarn pompons and fastened with a loop and large detail button.

note • each skein of linen yarn wraps two beads • the bigger the bead's hole, the more yarn can be wrapped around it, but remember to allow space for threading the beads onto a cord • use either a single colour or a combination of two colours held together to wrap each bead

wrap 28 beads. thread a large-eyed sewing needle with a long length of linen yarn. glue one end of the yarn to the outside of a wooden bead (A) with a dab of adhesive. pass the needle through the bead's hole and wrap the yarn tightly around the bead. repeat until the bead is completely covered. poke a knitting needle or bradawl through the bead's hole to open it up if necessary. cut the yarn, leaving a 1.5cm end. dab a little adhesive onto the end and push into the hole. allow to dry. repeat for each bead.

make two pompons 5cm in diameter and two pompons 3.5cm in diameter (see page 15).

cut a 100cm length of linen cord. tie a loop knot (see page 13) at one end to create a loop for fastening to the button (B). thread a wrapped bead onto the cord, passing it over the loose end of the loop knot to neaten. tie a simple knot in the cord close to the first bead. thread the remaining beads at random onto the cord, tying a knot between each bead to secure, until necklace is desired length. thread the button (B) onto the cord and tie as shown. tie on the pompons at random intervals.

materials

2 x skeins linen embroidery yarn, such
   as DMC Stranded Linen Thread, in
   each of the following colours: ecru,
   pearl, wheat, light pink, dusted pink,
   old rose, ochre, nut, burgundy

A 28 x medium (25mm) wooden ball
   beads, with 5mm hole

B 1 x large (35mm) button for fastener

large-eyed sewing needle

fine knitting needle or bradawl

PVA adhesive

1m linen cord for threading

69

linen, ribbon & fabric wrapped bead necklace

A pretty necklace made with lengths of linen skrim, printed ribbon and viscose thread, threaded with vintage buttons and a large wooden bead wrapped in embroidered silk. All assembled with an antiqued gold snap hook to fasten.

encapsulated beads & knitted tube necklace

This design uses an easy technique to create long tubes of knitting into which beads can be inserted. The stitches are worked on large needles in shimmering lurex yarn that encapsulates more shimmering beads of various sizes that stretch out the tube to give an open lattice effect.

encapsulated beads and knitted tube necklace

materials

For the bronze necklace:

1 x 25g ball lurex yarn, such as Rowan Lurex Shimmer or Yeoman Luxury Collection Starlight in bronze

22 gold ball beads – 5 x large (30mm), 10 x medium (25mm) and 7 x small (20mm) – or wooden ball beads spray painted to required colour

For the gold necklace:

1 x 25g ball lurex yarn, such as Rowan Lurex Shimmer or Yeoman Luxury Collection Starlight in gold

19 silver ball beads – 9 x medium (25mm) and 10 x small (20mm) – or wooden ball beads spray painted to required colour

pair 5mm double-pointed knitting needles
blunt-ended sewing needle

note • if you can't find metallic beads, use natural wooden ball beads spray painted gold or silver • the knots used in these necklaces are made using short lengths of lurex yarn, tied twice, very tightly, and on either side of each bead.

make knitted tube. cast on 6 stitches. knit 1 row. * slide the stitches along left-hand needle, without turning needles, up to the point. bring yarn across back of work from left to right and pull tightly. knit next row. repeat from * until work measures 75cm for bronze necklace and 80cm for gold necklace. leave stitches on safety pin with long end of yarn for grafting to cast-on edge.

for the bronze necklace: make a knot approximately 1cm from cast-on edge. insert a bead into knitted tube and push down. tie a knot tightly on either side of bead. repeat with all other beads until one bead remains. insert last bead into tube. join tube by grafting cast-on stitches and stitches from safety pin (see page 29). fasten off. tie across join.

for the gold necklace: make a knot approximately 2cm from cast-on edge. insert bead. tie tightly to enclose. make another knot 2cm further along tube. insert a second bead. tie tightly as before. continue adding beads, mixing sizes, leaving 2cm between each bead until tube is full. tie last bead. join tube by grafting cast-on stitches with stitches from safety pin as before. fasten off.

double button & glass bead bracelet

Choose classic fisheye buttons in toning shades and contrasting or clear glass beads to create a bangle that sparkles.

double button and glass bead bracelet

materials

1m black mercerised cotton thread
   (bootlace)
A 7 x large (22mm) fisheye buttons
B 12 x small (13mm) fisheye buttons
C 7 x medium (6mm) bugle beads
D 12 x small (3mm) seed beads
PVA adhesive

cut a 100cm length of cotton thread. fold in half to find the centre. thread the first large button (A) from the back over the two ends and move towards the folded centre. Do not thread right up to the centre but leave enough at the folded end to create a 5–6cm loop which will form the fastener.

hold the loop and large button in one hand, take the first strand and feed it back through the opposite hole. take the second strand, thread a bugle bead (C) and feed it back through the other hole. check the tension as you go.

take two small buttons (B), thread one onto the first strand and thread the other onto the second strand, topping each with a small bead (D). position the small buttons so that they nestle just beneath the larger buttons.

repeat until last button (A) remains. finish with a large button (A) and add bead (C). tie off with a reef knot on the diagonal so that it lies flatly and neatly. trim the ends. dab the knot and ends with PVA adhesive. allow to dry.

crochet & fabric wrapped bead necklace

Fabrics, yarn and ribbons in tonal hues of blues, basalt and burgundy, with flashes of fuchsia and turquoise are used to create this multi-crafted necklace. Beads are wrapped in printed fabric or basic double crochet.

crochet and fabric wrapped bead necklace

note • for basic instructions on crochet, see pages 17–23

wrap three large beads (A) and six medium (B) beads in assorted fabrics (see page 16).

cover 10 medium beads (B) with crochet – two in grey, four in burgundy and four in fuchsia. base ring with yarn and crochet hook, make 6 ch and join into ring with a slip stitch. round 1 1 ch, 10 dc in ring, slip stitch to first dc. round 2 1 ch, 2 dc in each dc to end of round, slip stitch to first dc. (20 dc.) round 3 1 ch, 1 dc in each dc to end, slip stitch to first dc. repeat rounds 3 four times. insert bead into crochet. next round 1 ch, [1 dc in next dc, miss 1 dc] to end of round, slip stitch to first dc. (10 dc.) repeat last round. (5 dc.) fasten off and sew in yarn ends.

tie a slip knot (see page 13) in one end of the rat tail cord. thread one large fabric bead onto the cord and position at the centre. tie a knot at each side of the bead to secure. thread another two large fabric beads, one at each side of the first bead, and knot. thread three medium fabric beads on each side and knot. thread five crochet beads on each side, with the last bead covering the starting slip knot. tie a slip knot at the other end of the necklace. poke the end of the cord through the hole of the last bead with the aid of a knitting needle. cut the ribbon in half and sew one half to each loop created by the slip knots. tie the ribbon ends together in a bow.

materials

oddments of fine-weight mercerised
    cotton yarn, such as Yeoman Cotton
    Cannele 4 Ply, in each of the
    following colours: grey, burgundy
    and fuchsia

2mm crochet hook

scraps of 1–5 different fabrics

A 3 x large (30mm) wooden ball
    beads, with 5mm hole

B 16 x medium (25mm) wooden ball
    beads, with 5mm hole

PVA adhesive spray

1.5m round satin rat tail cord

1m satin ribbon, 2.5cm wide

fine knitting needle or bradawl

sewing needle and thread

crochet flower, bead & button bag charm

A popular new accessory, the bag charm is a perfect project to personalise. Use a combination of handmade beads, covered n crochet and colourful printed fabrics. Contrast with vibrant buttons and a crocheted flower, all attached to a snap hook.

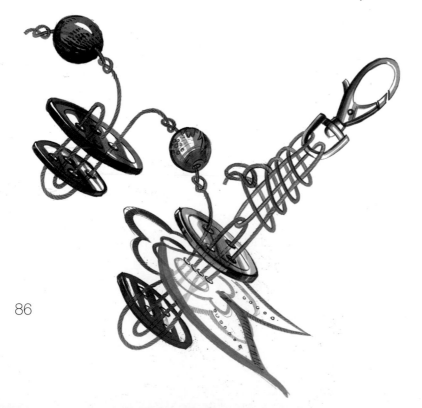

cover 1 large bead in crochet using yarn A. follow instructions given on page 84, but work three extra rounds at the centre of the cover.

wrap 1 medium bead in colourful printed fabric (see page 16).

make 1 crochet flower (see pages 17–23). base ring using yarn B and crochet hook, make 12 ch and join into ring with a slip stitch. round 1 1 ch, 18 dc in ring, slip stitch to first dc. round 2 1 ch, 1 dc in same place as 1-ch, 3 ch, miss 2 dc, [1 dc in next dc, 3 ch, miss 2 dc] 5 times, slip stitch to first dc. round 3 1 ch, [in next 3-ch loop work 1 dc, 3 ch, 5 tr, 3 ch, 1 dc] 6 times, slip stitch to first dc. change to yarn C. round 4 1 ch, 1 dc in same place as 1-ch, 5 ch, [1 dc between next 2 dc, 5 ch] 5 times, slip stitch to first dc. round 5 1 ch, [in next 5-ch loop work 1 dc, 3 ch, 7 tr, 3 ch, 1 dc] 6 times, slip stitch to first dc. fasten off and sew in ends.

cut out a leaf shape from the tweed fabric. cut a second leaf shape slightly smaller than the first. sew a row of ten bronze beads to each fabric leaf.

cut a 100cm length of cord. tie a knot in one end. thread the crochet covered bead and tie a simple knot to secure in position. leave a 2.5cm space. thread up through the back of the large button and the back of the small button, diagonally across and back down through both buttons, then back up through both buttons, then again diagonally across to make a cross-stitch detail and back down through both buttons, finishing at the back of the large button. leave a 2.5cm space then tie a simple knot. thread the fabric wrapped bead and tie a knot close to it. place the large purple button in the centre front of the crochet flower. arrange the two leaves behind the crochet flower, slightly overlapping. place the small yellow button to the centre back of the crochet flower. **thread** the large-eyed needle with the cord and pass up through the all the layers including the two buttons as given for the previous buttons, finishing at the back of the small button.

thread through the base ring of the snap hook, back down through the diagonally threaded yarn, across the back of the button then back through the base ring of the snap hook. **work** six slip knots down the length of cord to secure. **trim** the cord ends.

materials

for the crochet bead and flower:
oddment of fine-weight mercerised cotton yarn, such as Yeoman Cotton Cannele 4 Ply, in A fuchsia, B purple and C mauve
1 x large (30mm) wooden ball bead, with 5mm hole
2mm crochet hook

for the fabric bead:
scrap of colourful printed cotton fabric
1 x medium (25mm) wooden ball bead, with 5mm hole
PVA adhesive spray
fine knitting needle or bradawl

for the fabric leaves:
scrap of tweed fabric
20 x small (2mm) bronze seed beads
sewing needle and thread

to assemble:
1m pink round satin rat tail cord
1 x large (28–30mm) transparent pink plastic four-hole button
2 x small (15mm) transparent plastic four-hole buttons – 1 purple and 1 yellow
1 x medium (20–22mm) transparent purple plastic four-hole button
silver snap hook
large-eyed sewing needle

fabric flower, button & bead necklace

A very pretty and simple necklace to make. Hunt out embroidered vintage fabric and buttons in various styles, but all in the same colour to add impact. Alternatively, machine embrioder motifs that can be cut out of your chosen fabric.

fabric flower, button and bead necklace

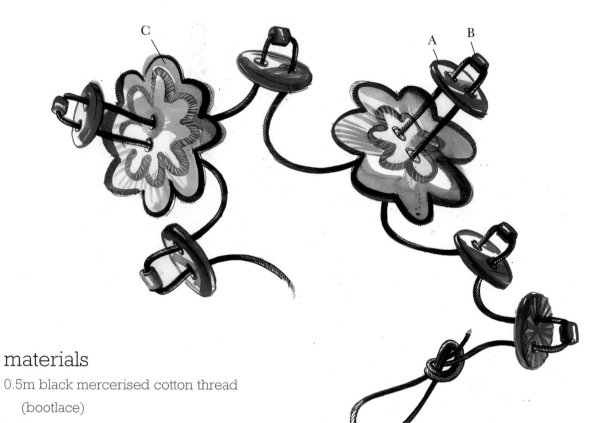

materials

0.5m black mercerised cotton thread
   (bootlace)

A 17 x assorted small (15–20mm) buttons

B 17 x small (3mm) glass seed beads in
   same colour as buttons

C 7 x fabric flowers (25–30mm) cut from
   embroidered fabric

fine hole punch

PVA adhesive

note • use an odd number of fabric flowers as it is important to have one that sits at the centre front • avoid threading the fabric flowers around the back of the neck as it will sit better

make two holes in the centre of each fabric flower (C) using a fine hole punch. cut a 50cm length of thread. arrange the assorted fabric flowers and buttons in the order that you want to thread them.

take the thread end and the first button (A) and thread up through the first hole. thread through a bead (B) then back down through the button. make a reef knot (see page 13) at the back of the button. thread the next button (A) with a bead (B) on top as before, leaving a 1cm gap between the first and second buttons. thread up through a flower (C) and up through a button (A). thread through a bead (B) then back down through the button and flower, leaving a 1cm gap between the preceding button and flower. continue to thread each button with a bead on top, leaving a 1cm gap between, and theading a flower with every other bead. continue in this way to the length required.

make a 5–6cm loop knot (see page 13) which will form the fastener. trim the ends. dab knot and end with PVA adhesive. allow to dry.

vintage

encapsulated glass bead & organza ribbon necklace

Fine wire mesh netting is threaded with large silver-grey glass beads, twisted with smaller clear beads, tied with grey organza ribbon and finished with a diamante buckle.

arrange the assorted beads in the order you want to insert them. **cut** a 50cm length of wire net tubing. **thread** the tubing through the first small bead (C) and position it slightly off centre to the right. **twist** the tubing on both sides of the bead to secure. **open** out the tubing and insert a medium bead (B) inside the tubing on each side of the first bead. **twist** to secure. **insert** a large bead (A) inside the tubing on each side. **twist** to secure. **thread** a bead medium (B) inside the tubing on each side. **twist** to secure. **thread** the tubing through a small bead (C) on each side. **open** out the tubing and insert a medium bead (B) inside the tubing on each side. **twist** to secure. **insert** a large bead (A) inside the tubing on the left side, but thread the tubing through a large bead (A) on the right side. **twist** to secure. **thread** a bead (B) inside the tubing on the left side only. **twist** to secure.

cut the organza ribbon into two lengths. **take** the wire net tubing on the left side, twist it together and make a loop knot (see page 13). **thread** the first length of ribbon through the loop knot and tie into a large sash bow. **fold** the second length of ribbon in half and loop it onto the loop knot, thread a small bead (C) over both ends, push up and tie a simple knot to secure.

pinch together the wire net tubing end on the right side and thread over the bar of the diamante buckle. **secure** with a few stitches using the sewing needle and thread.

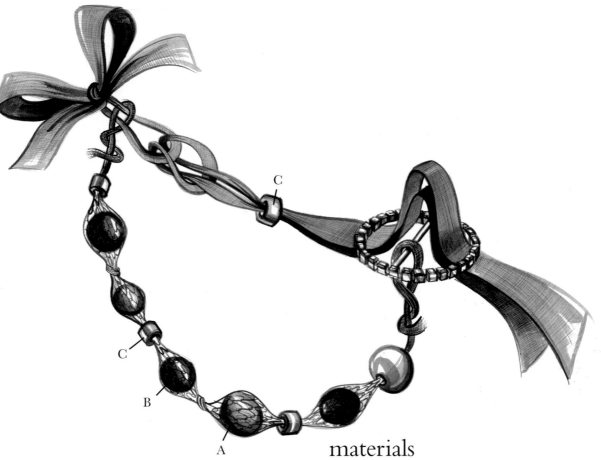

materials

1 x pack wire net tubing

A 4 x large (20mm) metallic silver
   glass ball beads

B 7 x medium (15mm) metallic grey
   glass ball beads

C 4 x small (10–12mm) metallic silver
   glass pony beads

1.5m organza ribbon, 2.5cm wide

diamante buckle, 3cm in diameter

sewing needle and thread

99

vintage button & glass bead pendant

An individual and original design using a selection of buttons, beads and a special button as a pendant and a little button to fasten. Any mixture of found or vintage beads and buttons can be used.

vintage button and glass bead pendant

materials

Approximately 1.5m black
mercerised cotton thread
(bootlace)

A 1 x large (31mm) mother-
of-pearl button

B 1 x small (15mm) mother-
of-pearl button

C 3 x small (6mm) black
faceted glass beads

D 4 x large (10mm) smoked
glass beads

E 1 x large (10mm) black
faceted glass bead

F 4 x small (5mm) black
faceted round glass beads

G 2 x small (4mm) black
five-sided glass beads

H 2 x small (3mm) matt
black pony beads

arrange the assortment of beads. **cut** a 150cm length of thread. **fold** the length of thread in half, then take one half and fold that in half again. **take** the large button (A) and push the second folded half of the thread through the top hole of the button from the front and pass the other ends through the folded half to secure. (You should then have one quarter of the length of thread to one side of the button and three quarters of the length of thread to the other side.)

thread one bead (C), passing both ends of the thread through the bead. **work** each end of the thread separately. **thread** one bead (D) onto each end of the thread followed by one bead (C), one bead (F), one bead (G) and one bead (H). **measure** about 22–23cm length of thread from the top of the threaded button and fold in half (you can adjust the length here if you prefer a longer necklace).

make a loop knot (see page 13) at this end to create a 1.5cm loop which will form the fastener. **pass** the working end of the remaining thread from this loop back through the threaded bead (H). **thread** a further bead (F) and bead (D). **pass** the working thread back through the threaded bead (C). **thread** one bead (E). **pass** the working yarn back through the next bead (C) on the other side of the necklace. **thread a** further bead (D) and bead (F). **pass** the working yarn back through bead (H). **make** a loop knot. **thread** the small button (B). **finish** with a reef knot (see page 13). **trim** the ends. **dab** the knots and ends with PVA adhesive. **allow** to dry.

crochet charm bracelet

A pretty and personal collection of vintage buttons, old leather buttons and glass beads are threaded onto a basic chain of crochet worked in viscose ribbon. The tones of amber, old gold, brass and chocolate brown are highlighted by the gold satin ribbon, which is tied as a final charm.

note • for basic instructions on crochet, see pages 17–23

make the crochet bracelet using a rat tail cord and a crochet hook. **begin** by making 31 ch (or length required plus 8 ch). **row 1** 1 dc in 8th ch from hook to create a fastening loop for large bead (H), then work 1 dc in each ch to end. **fasten off** and leave the tail ends for attaching gold bead (H) later.

thread each charm, button and bead (A–E) onto a jump ring, using sewing thread knotted onto each one. **thread** each small mother-of-pearl button (F) along with a glass bugle bead (G) onto a jump ring. **thread** the ribbon through a jump ring and tie into a bow. **attach** each decorated jump ring to the crocheted bracelet, staggering the rings along each side so that they will hang effectively, finishing with the ribbon bow close to the fastening loop. **attach** the large gold bead (H) to the end of the bracelet to act as the fastener.

materials

4m brown round satin rat tail
cord, 2mm thick

5mm crochet hook

12–15 assorted charms, beads
and buttons that can be
easily threaded, for
example:

A 5 x assorted large
(25–30mm) buttons,
including leather, mother-
of-pearl, vintage brass

B 1 x small (10mm) gold
glass ball beads

C 2 x medium (18–20mm)
natural stone beads

D 1 x medium (10–12mm)
gold ball bead

E 1 x large (18–20mm)
amber glass ball bead

F 2 x small (10–12mm)
bronze mother-of-pearl
two-hole buttons

G 2 x medium (18–20mm)
gold glass bugle beads

H 1 x large (15–20mm) gold
or gold painted ball bead

50cm satin ribbon, 15mm
wide

15 x gold jump rings

strong sewing thread

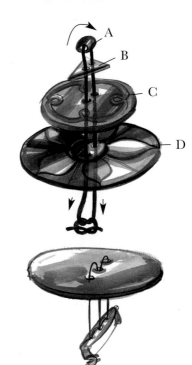

vintage button brooch

materials

1m linen thread
A 1 x small (2mm) seed bead
B 1 x small (10mm) triangular two-hole button
C 1 x medium (20mm) round two-hole button
D 1 x large (35mm) round two-hole button
scrap of leather
brooch bar pin
sewing needle
PVA adhesive

arrange the buttons one on top of the other in order of size, with smallest on top. **cut** a 50cm length of linen thread. **thread** through the seed bead (A). **thread** each end of the yarn through the front of the three buttons (B–D) in turn, finishing at the back of the large button. **tie** a reef knot (see page 13). **dab** knot with PVA and pull tight. **trim** the ends. **allow** to dry.

cut a 30mm disk of leather, using the large button (D) as a template. **cut** a 50cm length of linen thread and thread the sewing needle. **stitch** the brooch bar to the leather disk, placing it just above the centre, making sure that the thread ends are to the back of the leather disk. **tie** the threads off with a reef knot. **dab** knot with PVA. **trim** the yarn ends. **allow** to dry.

apply PVA to all the back of the leather disk. **place** leather disk on back of large button (D). **press** the leather disk and threaded buttons together. **allow** to dry.

art deco button bracelet

This double strand 'Art Deco' bracelet is made by threading one button, topped by another and finished with a bead.

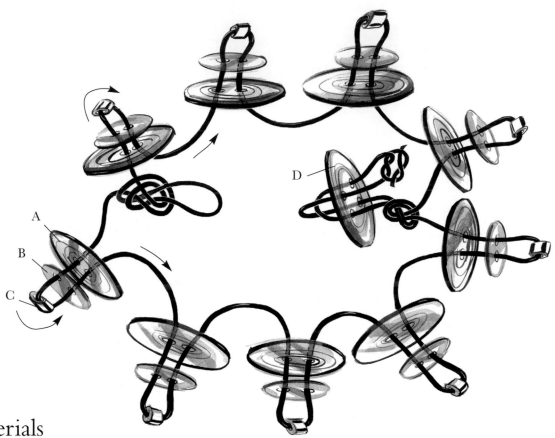

A
B
C
D

materials

Approximately 0.75m black mercerised
cotton thread (bootlace)
A 15 x medium (25mm) black and
white plastic two-hole buttons
B 15 x small (10mm) mother–of–pearl
two-hole buttons
C 15 x small (3–5mm) black and white
seed beads
D 1 x large (20mm) black and white
plastic four-hole button

cut a 75cm length of thread. fold the length of thread in half.
tie a loop knot (see page 13) at the folded end to create a
2–3cm loop which will form the fastener.

take the first strand. leave a 5mm space, *thread up through
medium button (A), small button (B) and bead (C), then back
through button (B) and button (A). take the other strand.
leave a 15mm space, and repeat from * for this side,
remembering to stagger the spacings of the buttons as you go
so that the buttons interlace.

make a loop knot (see page 13) using both ends and finish
by threading large button (D), taking the ends diagonally
through the hole. finish with a reef knot and cut the ends.
dab the knots and ends with PVA. allow to dry.

ribbon, sequin, lace & pearl button necklace

A necklace inspired by Edwardian parlour elegance. Silk ribbon, wide organza ribbon, sequins and lace are twisted and tied with random pearl buttons and tied in a decorative sash bow.

note • to make the necklace shorter or longer, simply cut the materials shorter or longer and use fewer or more buttons

thread the pearl buttons onto the organza ribbon, positioning one at the centre front and one at the centre back, with the rest evenly spaced in between. **tie** the ribbon in a flowing bow through the centre back button.

take the silk satin ribbon and weave randomly in and out of the organza ribbon. Tie in a simple knot at the centre back, allowing the ends to flow. **repeat** the last step this time using the lace. **repeat** the last step with the sequin strip but secure at the centre back through all the other ribbons.

materials

1.5m silk satin ribbon,
1.5cm wide

1.5m lace, 2cm wide

1.5m organza ribbon,
2.5cm wide

1.5m sequin strip

6 x pearl buttons with
loop shank

117

eclectic glass bead rope with silk tassel

An eclectic mix of large glass beads in jewel colours are threaded alternately with smaller faceted beads, which are complimented by matt black beads and contrasted by Oriental-inspired beads. A lush silk tassel finishes off this vintage-look rope necklace.

make a generous full tassel using black silk yarn wrapped around a 15cm length of cardboard (see page 14).

cut a long length of cotton yarn – much longer than required – fold in half and and loop through the uncut end of the tassel. **thread** both ends of the thread though the irregular bead (A), the Oriental bead (B) and a faceted bead (C), knotting each in turn. **tie** a simple knot. **work** on each side of the yarn in turn. **thread** a glass or plastic bead (D–L) and alternate with a faceted bead (C). **end** with a faceted bead (C) at the centre back. **tie** ends with a reef knot (see page 13). **thread** each end, in turn, back through this final bead (C) and through a few more beads, then tie in a simple knot.

materials

25g double-knitting-weight silk yarn, such as Debbie Bliss Pure Silk, for tassel

small amount of fine-weight mercerised cotton yarn, such as Yeoman Cotton Cannele 4 Ply

A 1 x large (30mm) black plastic irregular-shaped bead

B 1 x medium (20mm) Oriental-inspired bead or charm

C 22 x faceted smoked glass beads

D 4 x medium (20mm) grey glass pony beads

E 4 x medium (15mm) green glass seed beads

F 2 x large (25mm) grey glass bugle beads

G 2 x large (25mm) black plastic pony beads

H 2 x medium (20mm) purple glass ball beads

I 2 x medium (15mm) yellow square beads

J 2 x medium (20mm) grey oval beads

K 2 x medium (20mm) black plastic ball beads

L 2 x medium (15mm) bronze square beads

crochet amber pendant

A pendant necklace crocheted in lurex yarn. The 'pendant' is a large faceted amber stone enclosed in a net case, where the 'chains' are literally, two chains of crochet, one with little bronze beads worked in and the other, random crochet bobbles worked in together with larger faceted beads. The necklace is finished with extra ad-hoc button charms and an asymmetric bobble and bead detail.

note • for basic instructions on crochet, see pages 17–23 • to make the necklace shorter or longer, simply crochet fewer or more chains

using a 3mm hook, make 8 ch and join into a ring with a slip stitch. round 1 [5 ch, 1 dc in ring] 3 times, 5 ch, slip stitch to first ch of 5-ch loop. round 2 1 slip stitch in each of next 2 ch, [7 ch, 1 dc in next loop] 3 times, 7 ch, slip stitch to first ch of 7-ch loop. round 3 1 slip stitch in each of next 3 ch, [7 ch, 1 dc in next loop] 3 times, 7 ch, slip stitch to first ch of 7-ch loop. round 4 1 slip stitch in each of next 3 ch, [5 ch, 1 dc in next loop] 3 times, 5 ch, slip stitch to first ch of 5-ch loop. insert stone. round 5 1 slip stitch in each of next 2 ch, [1 ch, 1 dc in next loop] 3 times, 1 ch, slip stitch to first ch. fasten off leaving a long tail end of yarn to finish pendant.

thread 50 beads (A) onto yarn. using a 2.5mm hook, make a 70cm length of chain, adding beads randomly as you work. fasten off leaving a long tail end of yarn.

using a 2.5mm hook, work a few chains. work a bobble as follows – in second ch from hook work [1 dc, 4 tr, 1 dc]; then work more chains. continue to work random lengths of chain, randomly adding beads and working bobbles until chain measures 70cm. fasten off leaving a long end of yarn.

using a 2.5mm hook, work a few chains, make a bobble as given above in second ch from hook, then fasten off. attach it to the pendant with the tail end of yarn at the start of the chain and sew the other tail end of yarn into the bobble. make three more and attach in the same way.

take the length of the chain with the random bobbles together with the beaded chain. **lay** both chains out lengthways, ensuring they are the same length, then tie the ends together to create two circles. **attach** the remaining beads (B–C) and buttons (D) to the bobble group on the pendant to further embellish it. **attach** the pendant to the chains.

materials

1 x 25g ball lurex yarn, such as Rowan
   Lurex Shimmer

2.5 and 3mm crochet hooks

1 x large (50mm) amber stone

A approximately 100 x small (2mm)
   bronze seed beads

B approximately 6 x small (3mm)
   bronze faceted beads

C approximately 10 x medium (6mm)
   bronze faceted beads

D approximately 5 x small (5mm)
   mother-of-pearl buttons

approximately 25 x jump rings

125

sourcing beads & buttons

Beads are a constant source of inspiration in themselves. Chose from a huge variety of precious or semi-precious stones, crystal, pearl, glass, ceramic, wood, bone, and plastic, and in various colours, sizes and shapes, as long as it has a hole it can be threaded. Source from specialist bead shops, craft stores and even eBay; trawl thrift stores for vintage pieces and collect from clothing, bags and shoes; what you cannot find make by crocheting, knitting and wrapping with fabric, the only limitation is your own imagination.

UK

Bead Aura
3 Neals Yard, London WC2H 9DP
+44 (0)20 7836 3002
beadaura.co.uk

Brighton Bead Shop
21 Sydney St, Brighton BN1 4EN
+44 (0)1273 740777
beadsunlimited.co.uk

C&H Fabrics
179 Western Rd, Brighton BN1 2BA
+44 (0)1273 321959

Creative Beadcraft
20 Beak Street, London W1F 9E
+44 (0)20 7629 9964
creativebeadcraft.co.uk

Gartree Crafts
87 Largy Road, Crumlin, Co. Antrim,
Northern Ireland BT29 4RS
+44 (0)28 9442 2973,
gartreecrafts.com

John Lewis
johnlewis.com

J.T. Batchelor Ltd
9–10 Culford Mews, London N1 4DZ
+44 (0)20 7254 2962

Liberty
Regent St, London W1B 5AH
+44 (0)20 7734 1234
liberty.co.uk

Prym
Whitecroft, Lydney, Glos GL15 4QG
+44 (0)1594 562631
prymfashion.co.uk

Rowan
knitrowan.com

Scientific Wire Company
18 Raven Road, South Woodford,
London E18 1HW
+44 (0)20 8505 0002
wires.co.uk

V.V. Rouleaux
102 Marylebone Lane,
London W1U 2QD
+44 (0)20 7224 5179
vvrouleaux.com

Yeoman Yarns
36 Churchill Way, Fleckney,
Leics LE8 8UD
yeoman-yarns.co.uk

Yumyum Beads

3 Thorntons Arcade, Leeds,
West Yorks LS1 6LQ
+44 (0)113 244 2888
yumyumbeads.co.uk

France

La Droguerie

9 et 11 Rue du Jour, 75001 Paris
ladroguerie.com

US

DMC

77 South Hackensack Avenue,
Bldg. 10F, South Kearny,
NJ 07032-4688
+973 589 0606
dmc-usa.com

Lanaknits

Suite 3B, 320 Vernon Street,
Nelson, BC V1L 4E4
+888 301 0011 lanaknits.com

Purl

137 & 147 Sullivan Street,
New York, NY 10012
+212 420 8796, purlsoho.com

acknowledgements

This is a creative collaboration of many discerning and exceptional people.

Jane O'Shea – my editorial director and mentor, whose vision, style and encouragement have nurtured my career as a craft author. **Helen Lewis** – Creative Director, for her innovation and insight. **Lisa Pendreigh** – project editor and my rock, for her support, guidance and professionalism. **Claire Peters** – graphic designer, who is prepared to go the extra mile for design, my sincerest appreciation. **Diana Miller** – whose creative photography has captured craft and catapulted it into another realm. **Richard Merritt** – for his fabulous 'explosive' illustrations, which have transformed the 'how to' into the 'want to'. **Joy Fox** – whose personal style and work I have long admired since first we met at art school. **Sally Lee** – my creative practitioner for her enthusiasm, expertise and willingness to experiment.

And special mention and appreciation to **Mrs Pressy**, my first headmistress and needlework teacher – an inspiration. Not only did she become the first Lady Mayoress of Royal Windsor, but also inspired a shy and clumsy seven year old to love craft, AND undid her knots.

Projects by **Joy Fox** appear on pages 34–35, 48–51, 52–53, 78–81, 90–93, 100–103, 108–109, 110–113. For more information, email joyfox@mac.com

Editorial director Jane O'Shea
Creative director Helen Lewis
Designer Claire Peters
Project editor Lisa Pendreigh
Pattern checker Sally Harding
Photographer Diana Miller
Photographer's assistant Danielle Wood
Stylist Wei Tang
Illustrator Richard Merritt
Production director Vincent Smith
Production controllers Ruth Deary and Funsho Asemota

This paperback edition published in 2009 by
Quadrille Publishing Limited
Alhambra House
27–31 Charing Cross Road
London WC2H 0LS
www.quadrille.co.uk

Text and project designs © 2007 Erika Knight
Illustration © 2007 Richard Merritt
Photographs, design and layout © 2007 Quadrille Publishing Limited

British Library Cataloguing-in-Publication Data: a catalogue record for this book is
available from the British Library.

ISBN 978 184400 712 7

Printed and bound in Thailand